Stay Calm... You Can Do This!

The Journey to Single Parenting

Table of Contents

Preface and Acknowledgment

This is my first book to write, and the journey to this has been one of many phases. I am a single mother of one daughter, and I am proud to say that I have accomplished several of my personal goals through the experience of motherhood. I managed to raise my daughter with the help of my family and friends, while I worked to provide for the two of us. I have had full-time, part-time, and temporary jobs along the way, in addition to unemployment. I am proud to say I reached my goal of purchasing my first home, finally paying off my car, and making my educational goals a reality. Motherhood has been a hard road with many good times as I worked to make ends meet for my daughter and me. In the process of raising a child on my own, I received my Bachelor's degree in Business Management in 2008, and my Master's degree in Psychology in 2010 from the University of Phoenix online program.

Education is very important and I cannot emphasize enough how self-fulfilling the achievement was once I had received my degrees. I am so happy that I chose to go back and complete my educational goals. I put my education on hold to raise my daughter, and I always pondered the outcome had I completed my education in my twenties without walking away. I looked at my former classmates over the years and saw how they were achieving their career goals, while I was working in retail or temporary jobs with no degree. I will admit there was envy in my heart, as I wished I was in their shoes and able to enjoy the material things they had acquired. I knew my thinking was wrong, but I could not help the flood of emotions during those tough times.

My journey to writing this book has proven to be more insightful than I ever thought possible. After receiving my Master's degree, I decided to seek counseling for myself, so I could be sure I had worked through my own emotional struggles, and gain an understanding of how it feels to be counseled. My plan was to become a counselor who would sit behind a desk and meet with patients each week, but fate had other plans. Now I work to inspire other people to reach their inner peace. I make sure everyone I come in contact with or speak to has no doubt I truly understand the challenges they are facing. I've 'been there and done that.' I am not just a Psychologist who happens to be a single mother, but rather a single mother who happens to be a Psychologist.

In this book I want to speak from my heart and experiences as a single mother who struggled to make ends meet, and build a career. I want to share my perspective, as well as those of other single parents I have befriended along the way. Know that you are not alone in your situation, and that what you may be feeling or experiencing is shared among all single parents. Only the journey of how we became parents may differ. My struggles of not having enough money at times, lack of sleep, worrying daily, and wondering how the hell I was going to do all of this are only some of the circumstances I faced. There were times that all I could do was shake my head and live by faith. You can probably feel where I am coming from, and as you read this book, I want you to know that I get it… I really and truly get it.

I dedicate this book to my family, friends, and co-workers over the years. My family has been a tremendous help while raising my daughter, and although I had her out of wedlock, everyone supported me no matter what. My parents were instrumental in helping with my daughter, as they afforded me the opportunity to spend the first five years of my daughter's life at home with her. This is such a delicate time in our children's lives, and I was grateful to be able to spend this time with my child. My parents helped to give her a good foundation, and one that I will forever cherish. To my dear friend, Wanda, thank you for always telling me the unfiltered truth, no matter how much I did not want to hear it. Thank you to Sally and Mitzi for being there when I needed cheering up and support through all the ups and downs in my life. Thank you to Erma, Cassandra, Erica, Jose, Aubrey, Jamie, Ana, Jackie G., Theron, Charles A., and Christine for all the advice over the years, and especially for making me laugh when I really needed it most. To all of my family: Angela, William, Felicia, David, my mom (Delores), dad (James), my grandparents, Samantha, Tim, Devin, Daylen, Deja, and most of all my daughter, April. You all mean so much to me, and I appreciate everything that you have done in my life and bring to my life. When times were difficult, you all stepped in at one point or another to help me survive the seemingly insurmountable challenges of life. I will always cherish the support everyone gave me, and continue to give me, as I embark upon this journey of becoming an author. Thank you all for everything!

Introduction

Introduction

Where to begin? I have dreamed of writing a book for years, and finally through an emotional intervention, I am able to re-evaluate my life and what is truly important. Let me begin with the acknowledgement of understanding the hardships that single parents experience while raising kids. As a single mother of one, I can attest to the struggles that I experienced raising my daughter. Whether the option of having a child or children alone was by choice or not, the fact remains that single parenting is one of the hardest jobs around. Parenting (single or married) is a tough job and I applaud all who have stepped up to the responsibility.

After learning of my pregnancy, there were some fears about becoming a parent, and whether or not I would be a good parent to this child. Would I know what to do? How would I afford to pay for childcare? Finding out you are pregnant varies emotionally, depending on the person or persons involved. This can be exciting or traumatic for the expectant mother and father. In years past, single parenting carried a stigma, and many generations of people believed the notion of having a child out of wedlock was a sin, and ultimately viewed by many as unfavorable. Young women who found themselves with child were often sent away to alternative schools, or to live with relatives, so not to bring shame to the family name. In the twenty-first century, single parenting has become part of everyday life, if not part of the norm. Even though single parenting has become less of a taboo in society, the struggle of raising a child or children alone remains the same, if not tougher.

My experience draws from my life of raising a child alone, with support of family and friends. As parents, we try to raise our kids the best way we can, and of course we are going to make mistakes. You always hear people say, "there's no manual for raising kids, but if you find one please let me know." I truly can say that if I knew then what I know now, I would definitely make some different decisions. That being said, I would not be who I am as a parent had I not gone through the tough times of raising a child while working, going to school, maintaining a home, attempting to have a social life (one of the toughest of all), all while helping my daughter with her schoolwork and completing my own homework. Once I moved out of my parents' home and was on my own with my daughter, I did experience some tumultuous times that brought me to my knees and made me wonder if I could ever stand on my own two feet again.

I believe being put to the test of your will and faith, and surviving the trials of the test, is probably one of the surest ways to determine your true strength. The thought of giving up on trying to make it on my own in my apartment, or making a career for myself ran through my mind numerous times during the many struggles I faced. I would be lying if I did not say that I still encounter these feelings and emotions when difficult times happen. Early on, I experienced financial woes as I worked different jobs just to pay for my daughter's necessities. Though I was afforded the opportunity to live with my parents during my daughter's first five years, being a stay at home mom was as difficult and stressful as being a working mom. Being at home means taking care of all the chores, such as cleaning the house (which you expect to be totally clean all the time because you are home), errands to the grocery store, shopping for clothes for kids, and having dinner ready when everyone gets home. If anything, we put more pressure on ourselves to make sure everything is perfect, because we are home. And to some degree, other family members expect this, too.

When I first found out that I was pregnant, I was very scared and excited at the same time. I lived with my parents, and the thought of telling them I was pregnant at the age of twenty was pretty nerve racking. I remember telling my boyfriend, and his excitement about telling his family, but he also had reservations about breaking the news to my parents. I have a strong religious family background and I belonged to my maternal grandfather's church. My father became an ordained preacher in my teen years, and my paternal grandmother was a missionary in the church. And not to mention my dad's brother is a preacher and his two sisters were also deeply involved with the church. My mom's brother eventually became a preacher as well, and now leads the congregation at my grandfather's church.

   With this deep connection into religion came the beliefs that are associated with having a child out of wedlock. In the timeframe that I had my daughter, there was the shame in society of having a child and not being married. After telling my parents, they were not thrilled at the time, but accepted the situation. I dropped out of college to work full-time to pay for doctor visits and upcoming expenses of having a child. Eventually, I had to stop working due to physical concerns, and had to stop driving because I would fall asleep behind the wheel. I would be riding in a car with someone, and as soon as we went a few blocks, I would fall asleep. I remember one time when my sister and I drove a friend home to Shreveport, Louisiana, and as soon as we hit the highway from Fort Worth, Texas, I fell asleep and did not wake up until we arrived in Shreveport. We met her family and ate dinner before driving back with our friend's sister joining us, and again I fell asleep once we got on the highway and did not wake up again until we were back in Fort Worth. Everyone got a good laugh about that, including me. During my pregnancy, my daughter's father and I grew apart and tension grew between us regarding the pregnancy. The situation came to the point of me wanting to have the child, while he was confused about what he wanted. I am sure this was anxiety about the unknown, and we went through some intense discussions or arguments about it. During that time, I was scared of the unknown and harbored deep doubts as to how I would be as a mother and handle the responsibility of having a child. By the final month of my pregnancy, communication between my ex-boyfriend and me was minimal.

The day my daughter was born was one of the happiest days of my life. She was born on New Year's Eve, and I can vividly remember the doctors and nurses asking me if I wanted to prolong the birth until New Year's Day. I told them, "heck no!" I was understandably tired, but I also wanted the tax break. I remember lying in my hospital bed, staring at my new daughter, as my thoughts drifted to what life may have in store for us. Then I received a call from my sister, who was out with our friends and partying it up, and they called to say congratulations and wish me a happy New Year! Part of me was jealous that they were having fun at the party, but that quickly dissipated as I looked at the miracle in my arms. I knew I had plenty of time to party, but right now I had to focus on my future. Although I felt shame for having my daughter out of wedlock, and the relationship with my parents started off tense with the pregnancy news, I was blessed that my parents gave me the opportunity to be home with my daughter for the first few years. Many young girls do not have this kind of support, not only from their parents, but family, friends and even community.

Support System/
Work Life Balance

Support System/ Work Life Balance

A good support system is a necessity in raising children. For single parents, this cannot be a truer statement. Although I had my family and friends' support, there were numerous times where their help was not enough, because the help I needed was emotional. As mothers, we have to multi-task our lives around the kids, work, spouses (for some), family, school functions, and friends. This does not even include what we want to do for ourselves. We encounter moments of exhaustion and feeling overwhelmed, while attempting to balance it all. I remember going to the library, bookstores, and searching the internet for information relating to a support system for single parents. I found little to no resources to help me find other groups or organizations that specialized in assisting single parents. There are books on raising a child, what to expect with your newborn, work life balances and more, but none really touched on the needs of single parents. I know numerous people who are raising kids on their own. Through conversations, we learned that we all have experienced similar situations and felt the same emotions. After searching for information on resources for single parenting with no real success, I thought about writing a book from the perspective of a single parent and other single parents I had come to know. One major disadvantage we have is the work/ life balance issues. Most single parents are extremely dependent on daycare while they work, and have very little quality time with their child after work. The guilty feelings that arise due to lack of time spent with our child can be unbearable at times, but we have to continue to push on, because we are the only person upon which our child has to depend.

The support system for most single parents is limited, and selecting the best daycare can be quite a challenge. This is one area that is extremely difficult, because we have to implicitly trust those running the facility. In addition to struggling with trust, realizing that, due to our jobs, we do not have as much opportunity to drop by the facility to check up on them can add additional stress. I remember the first time I left my daughter at a daycare, and it was one of the hardest things I ever had to do in my life. I drove away crying, which continued for hours. Psychologists call this separation anxiety and I can honestly say that I felt every bit of it. Once I made it home, I immediately went out to the front yard and started hand watering the whole front yard while crying at the same time. People were driving by looking at me strangely, and I know that I looked a hot mess. But I felt like a hot mess at the time, because I was missing my daughter tremendously, and I had no control over my emotions. Each time I tried to stop crying, the tears came down even harder. Part of me felt horrible for leaving her there, but deep down I knew that she was in good hands, despite my out of control emotions.

After I calmed down, I had to realize that daycare was a reality, and one I needed to come to terms with, and quickly. Well that lasted all of one day. Ultimately, I chose to keep her home after a few days of daycare. It may or may not have been the best idea, but this was my decision. Looking back on it today, I would have kept her in daycare for the social skills, because all kids need to understand how to share and communicate with each other. If you're going through this right now, I would advise you to make an effort to let your child stay with friends or family members with young kids that you trust to care for your child for a few hours, so that you can adjust to being away from your child.

Our children are so important to us. Being away from them, especially our first born, is extremely difficult because we want to protect them from any harm. We believe the only way to do that is for us to stay by their side at all times. We scrutinize everyone who comes in contact with our children, so as to make sure he or she has our child's best interest at heart, which is true for most parents.

In our society today, working and balancing life outside of work has become one of the major topics that people stress over most. How to manage and get everything done on the list for the day, even when you have twenty items to complete, knowing only half of those items can actually be done within such a timeframe. You wake up in the morning rushing to brush your teeth, style your hair, shower, get dressed, and pack breakfast and lunch, and this is just your own routine. Then factor in making sure the kids and husband are awake and ready to go for the day. Life consists of running from one place to another, from the office to the grocery store, the cleaners, the daycare, the school, followed by a quick stop to a retail store and hardware store to check off the daily list. Once you make it home after a very busy day, then comes the household chores, schoolwork, kids' baths, dinner, putting kids to bed, and then quiet time for you around ten or eleven at night. For some, this time doesn't come until after midnight, or not at all.

One way to balance your personal and professional tasks is to find out what prioritization method works best for you. For example, a checklist, Microsoft® calendar (I prefer Google Calendar ™ because I can color code my appointments, tasks, and etc.) or even a journal may be ideal for you. I learned later in life that I worked best with a journal, and I put tabs on pages where I have active projects or tasks. Give it a try!

Years ago…life was somewhat slower and more relaxing for families. There was time to wake up late with the windows open in your home, everyone waking up to the refreshing air and he or she would leisurely go about his or her day. Kids played outside more without the threat of someone kidnapping them or harming them in any way. They were able to run up and down the residential streets to friends' homes and the whole neighborhood watched after the kids. No one panicked about the whereabouts of the kids, because they knew they were at one of their friends' homes and was taken care of, fed, or entertained. Today, danger lurks around every corner, and we have to watch our children closely when they go outside to play. Playing in the backyard of your home is not a safe place anymore, as predators are breaking into our "safe zones" and taking our children. Please always be aware of where your children are, because our precious little people are depending on us to protect them.

Today, working is absolutely necessary, and for many, to maintain a home requires two incomes. This necessity creates stress at levels for which we are often not prepared. Knowing that the loss of a job could create such financial hardship, causing the loss of all that you have achieved, is too frightening to fathom. But it is this fear that keeps us going each day, striving to make it a better day than the day before, to complete another goal or challenge, to support our family and kids the best way we know how, and to do our best to make it to work every day. All the pressure that we put upon ourselves to be the best, not wanting to fail our families and children, can become quite overwhelming. We have to make sure we put everything that is happening in our lives into perspective. Many times we stress about the little things that seem enormous to us at the time, but in all actuality they are just a very small part of our day or decisions.

We should be concentrating our efforts on the bigger issues in our lives, and determine how important these issues are to us. Only then can we figure out if the resolution of the smaller problems can wait, while we concentrate on other problems that are more pertinent at the present time. As women and men, I know we look at the whole picture, but in so doing, the whole world seems too complicated, and at times unbearable. We have to learn to take issues one at a time, and to live in the present without focusing so much on what will happen tomorrow, the next day, the next day after that, or even a few months from now. Here are some examples of ways to gain some control in your life and keep your sanity:

- Prioritize what needs to be done today. Then, narrow down the list to what can actually be completed in your schedule.

- Create a routine for yourself and include the kids' schedules in your routine. This helps to make sure you are taking care of you too. Make sure to add some "me time" into your routine so it will become a habit, rather than feeling like a chore.

- Utilize the calendar in your email account to input all of your tasks and everyone's schedules, then sync the calendar to your cell phone. This will help you stay organized. And if you set up a generic account, everyone (spouses, kids and grandparents) you give permission to can access the calendar and anticipate events.

- Make sure to calm down before making big life decisions. You do not want to make a rash decision based on your emotions, especially if you are upset.
- You will make mistakes. But always remember that everything can be fixed.

Asking for help is another issue that we as single parents struggle with and are reluctant to do, because of the threat of feeling like a failure or the appearance of being weak. These feelings can be overwhelming, and potentially hamper us when we need assistance the most. But when you look at the bigger picture, you will see that asking for help actually demonstrates your strength from within. We are stronger than we realize, because we are able to make what feels like the impossible happen. You know what I mean, when we are down to our last dime and still have to figure out how to buy food and gas, and yet somehow we find a way to provide. Looking back at the times I managed to overcome the money struggles, I still wonder where the money came from, considering my budget on paper never left anything extra. Then I remembered that God would take care of my family and me. I was able to work at a store that allowed me to cash my check in the store, as long as I spent at least half of my earnings on goods from the store. And that certainly was not a challenge, as I had to buy formula, diapers, and everything else my daughter needed. Once I realized that asking for assistance was not only okay for me to do, but beneficial, I then began to talk with co-workers. I realized that some of them were raising kids on their own as well, which was such a surprise to me. We all were going through similar problems, and we quickly realized that each of us had different ways of handling various issues. One of my co-workers asked family members to help with taking care of the kids while she worked, and in return they lived with her while they attended college. My advice is to talk with other people, because they may have ideas that you have never thought about or even considered. I drew inspiration and ideas from my friends and co-workers, hearing their experiences and how they handled struggles and difficult times. I learned not to sweat the small things. I had heard this saying throughout my life, but it did not hit home until I was overwhelmed by my financial issues and busy schedule, and I realized I was stressing too much on the small stuff. I will admit that letting the little things go certainly was not easy, because I tend to worry and stress about everything. I tend to overanalyze things, and many of my friends graciously pluck me back into reality. So do not give up when your back is against the wall and you are faced with hard times.

We are stronger than we ever thought we could be when it comes to our children. If we will fight and do anything to protect them, then why not do the same for ourselves? If we don't fight for ourselves, then we diminish our inner strength to keep pushing through each day. Our children need us. So we, as parents, need to seek assistance, advice, and help in any way possible to ensure we give them the best parent we can be. If you have no one to talk to, try starting your search at your church or place of business. Some work places provide Employee Assistance Programs (EAP) that can put you in touch with someone who can assist you in various areas.

The daily struggle of wondering if I am good enough, if I am doing the right thing, or if I can take much more is something that weighed heavy on my mind as I raised my daughter. How many times have you fallen to your knees, or cried yourself to sleep, unable to answer these questions? Even though my daughter is grown, I know I still wonder today if I am making the right decisions, and there are still challenges we both face. We have to realize that the old saying, "God does not put more on us than we can bear," is true, and we have to find that inner strength and faith to know that we can make it through any challenge that comes our way. During these difficult times, we have to remember to take time out for ourselves (the "me" time). Even if it's only thirty minutes per day, make sure you do something that helps you relax and continue to dream for your future. Go get a massage, see a movie, exercise, or schedule quiet time at home to rest. Also, I urge you to find true confidants who know what you are going through, so you have a safe place to ask questions, solicit their advice, or just vent.

My mother gave me some invaluable advice early on, which was to sleep when the baby is sleeping. I know... you are probably wondering how you are going to accomplish the cleaning, the laundry, or whatever chore you have on your lengthy list for the day, if you allow yourself to collapse on the couch for two hours while the baby sleeps. I told my mom the same thing and I quickly understood why she told me this outstanding bit of wisdom. If you are slaving away to get things completed while the baby is sleeping, then when he or she wakes up, you are even more tired than before. And as a result, the baby is well rested. Honestly, this is when your patience is depleted, and the chance of losing your temper is considerably higher. Be very careful not to take it out on your child, no matter how high the emotions run. On the other hand, if you sleep when they sleep, then you are both well rested, and they are more likely to stay pacified with a toy or just watching you while you are cleaning. Trust me on this and give it a try.

As a single parent trying to work for a living, it is imperative to develop a daily plan to stay organized and allow for quality time with your kids, getting chores done, bathing kids and getting them to bed, and even some quiet time for yourself at the end of the day. To be honest, it took quite some time for me to grasp and implement this, but it certainly is possible. I never understood when other parents would show up to work and proclaim their job was their getaway. But now I understand completely! A lot of times when my daughter was younger, I viewed work as my getaway as well. It made sense, because at work, I had additional support and help with the duties that were required each day. There was a team to share the workload, but I only had myself to complete the workload at home. But how can we say we need more help at home?

Balancing the job and home is tricky, and truthfully it can be frustrating. The job pays the bills and provides for the family. But essentially spending most of your day at the job means less time with the family. So when is enough? How do you set boundaries on the hours that you will dedicate to working, and the rest of the day to your family, as well as yourself? My advice: don't take your work home with you. This will allow you to switch gears easily at night when you stroll through the door, so you can take care of home and family. If you must bring work home, then only schedule a short allotment of time, and try to complete it over the weekend, if possible. Try to keep your weeknights free for quality family time. And remember not to forget to take time for yourself! I admit that I still have problems remembering to take care of myself first. Each day is a conscious effort to make sure I do something for me. I know that I get caught up in my busy life, and there are times when I feel guilty for not spending more time with my daughter, friends, and family. I know now that I cannot be helpful and productive for others if I am not at my best. So taking time for me to relax or doing something that I enjoy is a way to rejuvenate myself, which aids in remembering the happier and less stressful times in my life. Most of the time, the "me" time meant taking a long, hot bath and quieting my mind of the day's issues. I know that trying to alleviate your thoughts and worries is easier said than done. The process will take practice. First, concentrate on something that makes you relax and be at peace. For me, this is a lazy day at the lake on a partly cloudy day, when the water is still, as I take in the fresh air and calmness around me. What makes you feel relaxed? Imagine it and practice retreating to your quiet place until you can do it with ease. This works great at work when you need a moment to relieve some of the stress. Take a few minutes at your desk or sit in the car at lunch and focus on the quiet moments. While we have to deal with stress and taking care of ourselves through the stress, let's not forget the emotional roller coaster that we all experience as single parents.

Single Fathers

Single Fathers

Though I write this as a single mom, I know that there are countless single fathers out there who are doing their best to raise their children. For the fathers who have accepted the responsibility of taking care of your children alone, you should feel proud you have embraced this amazing responsibility that so many men have not. Many men do not honor their responsibilities as fathers to do everything in their power to protect and provide for their family. This creates a pseudo stereotype that many men do not own up to and accept what they have helped to create. This belief has created a hardship for men to be accepted by women who have encountered negative experiences with other men. So in turn, when a good man comes along, it can be arduous for many women to see the good shine through. The inability to overcome stereotypes and welcome a good man is merely a result of trust issues from past relationships. But remember guys, there is a woman out there who will accept you for who you are and love your children as their own.

Although both men and women experience trust issues, we hear most often from women, which is what the media typically displays. We hear a lot about people not making their child support payments, not visiting their children, and completely walking away from their responsibility. Perhaps some men withdraw from their parenting responsibility because of drama ensuing between him and the mother of his children. Women... you know how we can be! While we want to protect our kids, we have to remember our children need their fathers as well. As women, we must dismiss our personal feelings, good or bad, toward the fathers for the sake of our children, to appropriately parent. We should not use how we feel as an excuse to withhold him from his children. In addition, never talk negatively about your child's father in front of your child. Your own hurt feelings have nothing to do with your child's feelings toward their father. Let your child make their own mind up about their fathers, as they get older and build a relationship with him. This advice is true to men and women alike.

In present day, men and women have stepped up to the plate and owned their responsibility as parents to ensure their children will develop into healthy and prosperous young adults. I give credit to those single men who have taken on the job of taking care of their children by themselves. Through conversations, a good friend of mine acknowledged that this was both the best and hardest decision he ever had to make. Raising kids without a lot of knowledge of caring for an infant is a challenge for any man or woman. And society has depicted men as providers and women as nurturers, so most men believe it isn't in their nature to care for children, especially on their own. I truly admire my friend for taking on the responsibility, seizing the opportunity to step up, and doing a phenomenal job of raising his children.

If you are a single man parenting alone, make sure you take the same advice and ask for assistance. The pressure of raising kids is substantial, and carrying the stress and emotion inside (as many men have the tendency to do) can lead to a total breakdown. Or worse, you may voice your frustration on your kids, which is not ideal or productive. Find opportunities for your "me" time. This could be asking family members to watch the kids for a day or overnight so that you can rejuvenate yourself. Use this time to accomplish some things you may have been putting off or couldn't make time to complete. And remember, you are not alone, as there are many men who have also taken on the vigorous task of solo parenting. Research the internet or ask your church community for support groups where single fathers can come together and support each other. I want to recognize those single men who are co-parenting and making sure your children are taken care of, as well as being an intricate part of their lives. I know it's not easy to remain positive, amidst the preconceived ideas as to what men will and will not do for their kids. Many men are dealing with ex-girlfriends who have a problem getting past the break up, and in turn use the kids as pawns to control the time or activities involving the father and his children. This action is indisputably wrong, but adds to the ongoing emotional roller coaster.

Emotional

Rollercoaster

Emotional Roller Coaster

Now to the emotional side of things...yes, we do have emotions and they do matter! We all go through a wide range of emotions as we raise our kids, and this is a natural part of life. As single parents, however, we don't have that significant other to step in to help when we are having a bad day or not feeling well. We embody both mother and father, and often times there just isn't time for a day off. Because we feel almost "on call" all the time, feeling overwhelmed seems to be the new norm. And although we know this is not acceptable, candidly, it's all we know. We venture into the role as parent, yet we are rarely prepared for what is ahead of us. Raising kids is not done by a playbook, but more so by the seat of your pants. Had you known before you had kids that you would be tested emotionally and physically, probably every single day, you would not have believed it. You might have said, "whatever... I am in control and my kids are not going to act like some of these other kids that I see acting out around here." Yeah right! Even though we may raise our kids with the best intentions, eventually their own personalities take over and they will make good decisions, bad decisions, or even huge mistakes. They may test every last nerve. But when you see your newborn for the first time, your eyes light up and a smile spreads from ear to ear. The pure joy of holding your newborn is simply elating and softens even the hardest heart. I remember holding my daughter in my arms for the first time, and being utterly amazed this beautiful child was mine. As I studied each precious feature, I found myself giddy, for she resembled me! I was overcome with mixed emotions, as I imagined life with my new daughter, and what the future held for us. One moment I found myself happy and excited, and the next moment feeling utterly scared of what was coming our way next. I went back and forth on those emotions for months. I honestly had no idea I could love someone so much until I held that baby in my arms following the delivery. Quite frankly, those feelings kept me going each day, providing fuel to fight the struggles that came my way. It was my fears of trying to figure out how to support my daughter and where my own life was going which scared the crap out of me, but I would not change anything because the experience was well worth it.

Watching new parents is wonderful, seeing the love in their eyes that comes purely from their hearts, as they show off their children. It's awe-inspiring to see the proud fathers with their chest out as people acknowledge their children, and they realize they had a hand in creating this child. Many struggle with being too protective of their first born child, so much so they hesitate letting others, even family members, take care of them even for a brief moment. Then we learn later on that it is okay to let go for a bit, just to have some much needed time for you. That is a lesson that we all have to learn as we raise our children. True, being a protective parent is noble, but as mothers, we must learn boundaries. I know single dads also experience the same emotions, so this is a great reminder for all of us.

As a new mom, no advice is good enough. We believe we are the only one who knows what's best for our child and how to take care of them. I remember my mom and other friends whom are mothers telling me what I needed to do, but I was not eager to listen. I thought I knew it all back then. Of course, I quickly learned that I didn't know it all.

The colds and flus that go around can be dangerous for infants and toddlers, so being protective of our kids is not always a negative thing. Just trying to keep our own hands clean and sanitized can be a job in itself. It seems everyone you meet wants to hold your child, and you find yourself cringing as they kiss on them and fondle their little hands and feet! Unfortunately, all we see as parents is a potential sick child, with no sleep for anyone in the house. Times are challenging enough with a well child, so sickness has a tendency to stretch everyone to their limits. I clearly remember the many sleepless nights with a feverish and coughing little girl who couldn't get comfortable. I also remember rocking her to sleep in my arms so I could get some rest sitting up in the chair. Ahhh the memories!

I know the feeling of going to work with little to no sleep, trying to function at work, let alone stay awake. I lovingly referred to this as the 'walking zombie phase!' I would have to get up and walk around, or make numerous trips to the restroom to put water on my face. Sometimes I would just sit in the stall and close my eyes for a moment, or escape to the car during lunch and sleep for a bit to appear functional. The problem with sleeping in the car is just making sure you do not over sleep, because you don't want your co-worker or boss knocking on the car window to wake you up. I'll admit it did happen to me once, but fortunately no one noticed I was gone longer than normal. (I recommend setting an alarm on your phone.) The day this happened to me, my daughter had been sick for several days, and she was unable to sleep because she was coughing a lot. With only four hours of sleep in 48 hours, truthfully, I was fading fast. Unfortunately, this zombie-like state became a normal way of life, and I learned to adapt to functioning under immense exhaustion. I know working under such extreme conditions are not ideal, but that was my reality. And with the fatigue also comes the inability to control your emotions. I remember cycling through a range of emotions from rage, frustration, guilt, joy, sadness, happiness, anger, denial, and acceptance of the trials and tribulations. During these moments, I had to let myself feel the emotion, and know that it was okay to have these feelings. The important piece for me was to confront them head on, and not hold them in until they exploded later. And even if we do break down or explode, it's important to forgive ourselves and move on. I survived, and so will you.

A single parent wears many different hats. And when looked at as a whole, the many hurdles would bring even the strongest person to their knees. We have all sacrificed something to raise our children. For some, this is our identity; we are now known as this person's parent or this person's spouse. When asked who I was, I would respond with, 'a mother' or 'a daughter.' When I was truly pressed for a deeper expression of who I was, I could not answer it. Honestly, I had no clue who I truly was, for I had gotten lost in the worldliness of it all. Losing ourselves is surprisingly easy to do, because we are so caught up in the daily chores and issues that need our attention. In turn, we put ourselves on the back burner and forget to return to that burner. I was known merely as my father's daughter, or my daughter's mom, and I constantly asked myself when I would be able to do what I wanted to do.

I remember the moments of crying that uncontrollable, ugly cry. This happened when I had been pushed to my breaking point, and the tears ran down my face and I just could not stop them. Often it was during a night when my daughter was sick and unable to sleep, and even once I'd gotten her back to sleep, she would wake up coughing continuously and crying. I knew she was tired, too, and I had schoolwork of my own to do, along with working a full-time job. Trying to handle all of that on my own stressed me beyond my limits, bringing me to my knees many times over the years. Numerous times the tears would start falling at work, which is almost impossible to conceal. And just one person stopping by my desk and asking me, "How are you today?" would prompt me to burst into tears. Sometimes, once the tears started falling, there was no end to them, and many times I was thankful to have a sympathetic boss whom was a single parent as well. We helped each other through those times and formed a close bond. Not everyone is fortunate enough to have a boss who truly gets it, and who can connect on that emotional level, or even understand it for that matter. I highly recommend taking personal time off from work to face personal issues, because I finally decided to reach out for help and get counseling. It is sad that our society has shunned those who sought therapy, perpetuating the stigma that all who ask for help have psychological problems. Now, counseling can be a vital tool to help you figure out what is going on in your life emotionally, and why you make the decisions that you do in your friendships, relationships, jobs, and financial situations. I am confident that counseling was a divine intervention in my life. It was the best decision that I ever made for my personal health, and I encourage all to seek that emotional support while raising children, because the physical toll can be grueling to your mind and body.

Physical Tolls

Physical Tolls

There is a lot to say about the physical toll that parenting can have on someone. The lack of sleep makes you drag around all day. I would become forgetful, even to the point my boss would tell me to do something and I would jump up from her desk and head right next door to mine, and forget everything she had just asked me to do. I kept getting frustrated with myself, because I knew I was better than that, and it was incredibly embarrassing to have to go back to ask her what she wanted me to do. Then the headaches would start, because I was trying so hard to remember all the things I needed to do each day. Factor in the constant yawning with watery eyes... barely able to see the computer screen through the tears running down my face. And my eyes so red people thought I was not feeling well or clearly upset over something.

The lack of energy slows you down considerably, and you continue to push through it all with energy drinks, vitamins, excessive coffee, and whatever else to keep you going. I've spoken with other single parents, and the story is the same. We all have pushed so hard, the fatigue causing us to fall asleep everywhere. I can easily remember falling asleep standing up, at my desk, even while driving home after work while sitting at traffic lights. It didn't matter wherever I happened to be at the time; my body said to me, "what do you think this is, I cannot do anymore!" When you get to this point, you know that you truly need help, and yet you are paralyzed when trying to find it. Remember to take that "me" day as often as you can, and preferably during the week. Take the kids to school or daycare as usual, then go home and go to BED! Get several hours of sleep first, and then do some chores if you need to, but don't overdo it. Otherwise, you will be right back where you started.

When you are rundown, physically, it seems as though you are falling apart at a young age. There are parts of your body that suddenly hurt, and you did not even know you had a muscle there. I had to laugh at myself over the years, because I was young, and yet sounded like I was going on ninety the way I would move and complain about my physical ailments. I would look at my mom and grandmother, who were very active, and they would run circles around me, and I can still say that today. I could never figure out how they kept going and going, even waking at four in the morning each day. I was certainly not thinking about getting up that early, let alone opening my eyes that early to even see what time it was, so I have to give them props for being able to get everything done each day. I have memories as a child of my mom and grandmother cleaning their kitchens every night before going to bed. They would wash and dry the dishes, thoroughly clean the stove, sweep the floors, and even mop the floors each and every night. This was in addition to working full-time and coming home to cook dinner and tend to all of us. Today, I barely have enough energy to cook and wash the dishes after work, let alone sweeping and mopping the floor. In order to push through each day, we have to motivate ourselves to get up each morning and accomplish what we can for that day, and accept the results as the day ends. Some days will be more difficult than others, but we have to move on for the sake of our kids. You have to dig deep, keep pushing forward, and take each day one step at a time.

Self-Motivation

Self-Motivation

Keeping yourself motivated on a regular basis can be challenging, even if you only have yourself to inspire. But if you have to motivate your kids and yourself, this can be defeating at times. There seems to be no down time for single parents, working an eight or more hour shift, only to come home and deal with the daily grind and expectations of managing a household. We constantly hear that all we need to do is step out on faith and everything will be okay. But having faith and releasing all the stresses and worries is sometimes easier said than done! Our human nature is to worry and stress about everything, but too much stress is bad for our health, and we cannot be strong for our kids if we are sick ourselves.

'Sickness' can present itself as stressed out, heart issues, high blood pressure, depression, weight issues (anorexia, bulimia, or excessive weight), or insomnia. The list goes on and on regarding health issues related to stress. We have all experienced the struggles of life, but it is time that we find what motivates us from within or deep into your inner core. Does seeing your kids smiling faces motivate you? Is it when you accomplish a goal, no matter how small? How about making a plan for your future, and seeing yourself make it one step closer to achieving it? Do you repeat positive affirmations to encourage yourself each day? The last question is a pertinent one, because if you do not believe in yourself, then no one else can or will. You have to build up your confidence and learn to accept yourself as you are.

Accepting yourself as you is huge! As parents, we all find faults in ourselves. We are quick to pile on the faults when we focus on our family, and we blame ourselves for the situation that we are in. There are numerous issues that we cannot control, and yet still we believe it is our fault. Whenever there is an issue and we are struggling through something, we need to learn to see the issue as a learning experience. Determine what the lesson is, and do not repeat it in the future. I struggled with this as well, because I would wallow in pity for myself, instead of working to find out what lesson I needed to learn. I usually only had to repeat a lesson once before I got it, because it was difficult going through them over and over again. Why do we continue to repeat our problems before we recognize them? Everyone around you who believes in you and supports you can easily see when you are involved with the wrong person, when you are making bad decisions financially, and when you continue to fall for any excuse a person gives you when they do not have your best interest at heart. We least suspect family members as causing us harm or steering us in the wrong direction. Depending on family dynamics, it may be surprising who is truly committed to helping you grow as a person and follow your path to a promising future. Many people will help you achieve your goals, but there are those who are not able to support you, because they are struggling with their own feelings of not being able to accomplish more. And seeing you moving in the right direction can be difficult for them to accept and support.

Although you may experience criticism from other people, please remember that you are an individual and you have to decide for yourself the direction you want your life to go. Receiving constructive criticism can be a guide to assist you in finding your path to your personal goals. Do not accept criticism that puts you down or makes you feel less than a person. For example, being told, "you can't do that," "you don't know how to do that so try something else," or "it's too late for you to go back to school," are just a few examples.) This type of criticism is not constructive, because the motive is to get into your head and make you doubt yourself. When you begin to doubt your decisions and yourself, find a quiet place to gather your thoughts without the interference of others, or 'noise in your ears,' (as I like to say.) You need to focus on what you want to do and the decisions you need to make.

If you feel you need help getting motivated, then look within yourself for strength, talk to a true confidant or counselor, or read self-help books. If you have health issues, then seek a doctor's assistance, or go exercise and focus on yourself. Getting yourself healthy can be a powerful affirmation to know that you look and feel great. Always remember to work on yourself, because you are important.

Elementary Years

Elementary Years

The infant and elementary years are the most precious times that we have with our children, because these are the years that our kids truly need and want us to be around. These years are also filled with many ups and downs, as we try to maneuver our way through parenting and learning many things along the way. There are no parenting guides out there to prepare us for the reality of life and all the struggles and sacrifices that come along with it. This is one of those times when people who are already parents try to tell you what to look forward to, or tips on raising your child. One experienced parent gave me a warning about temper tantrums. I was told not to be surprised if my child bursts into a full-blown temper tantrum in the middle of the floor of a busy retail store, especially after you've told them they can't have that toy they have been looking at while you were perusing the clearance rack for clothes. Then watch the reaction from people witnessing the event, waiting to see how you're going to respond. Unfortunately, there may be someone lurking nearby, just waiting for you to discipline your child the wrong way (in society's opinion) and call Child Protective Services (CPS) to file a report of abuse or neglect. It's disappointing that fraudulent reports account for a large percentage of these calls. And as if we aren't stressed enough about doing or saying the wrong thing, how about the first time your child repeats something they heard at home (parents, TV or other sources) that's inappropriate right in front of strangers in a store or at church? I'm still astonished how young kids can use words correctly when they don't have a clue what they mean. And what do you say when your child asks where babies come from? That one catches all of us off guard. From experience, first remember to calm yourself and think before you speak. Most kids don't know much and are just curious because another kid mentioned it, maybe on the playground. So before answering, ask them what they know about it first, and then explain it to them on their age level.

Take advantage of the vast knowledge around you that you may find in your grandparents, parents, friends, relatives, and people in your community. You do not have to follow everyone's advice, but at least it gives you a good foundation. Not every parent out there is a good parent, and most believe that they are the best parent. Use your best judgment and take the advice of the people who most affect or influence you in a positive way. Each child's personality is different. And how you teach them or discipline them will be different as well. One child may respond by your taking away his or her favorite toy, while another may need to be placed in timeout. Pay close attention to each child's learning style, because this is a great source for you to know to discipline the most effective way. For instance, some kids are more visual, and need to see what the consequences or rewards are to their behaviors. Others can be told of the consequences and rewards, and for them, this is just as effective. Our decisions during this time affect our kids greatly, as we are their primary influence. Most of our influence is through our own actions, versus the words we say to our kids. If you say one thing and then do another, kids tend not to take you seriously, nor have respect for you. So whatever you do... stick to your word, show them the right way, and demonstrate how to respect others. The respect starts at home, because we have to learn to respect our children as well. Although they are young people, they still have their own minds, and we want to keep them pure.

We have to challenge them at every point, which means staying one step ahead of them in education and in life. Education is one privilege that we as Americans sometimes take for granted, because we live in a country with access to endless options and opportunities. It is because we have this access that we tend not to seek more. Our children deserve the best in life, and an education is one way to achieve that goal. Some parents did not have a good parent to show them the way or challenge them, or perhaps they did not have a parent at all. If this sounds familiar to you, it is even more important that you take the time to improve yourself and learn more about the things you do not know or even the things you always wanted to know. As a stronger and more knowledgeable person, you become a positive influence on your children.

These early years are trying for sure. Staying up all
night with sick kids or crying your eyes out because you are so
overwhelmed, creates that feeling that you have no idea what to
do or what move to make next. There were the times I didn't
know how I would pay the bills, put gas in the car, pay for
groceries, make car repairs, pay rent or my car payment.
Numerous times I struggled to afford school clothes, and still
have enough to pay for the field trips my daughter was looking
forward to, because all of her friends were going. And there
were always items needed for extracurricular activities, such as
sports, music lessons, etc. I know… OH how I know what you
are going through! There were many nights when I felt there
was nowhere to go or no one to call on to help me. Many of
those nights I prayed and cried myself to sleep, as I did not want
to disappoint my daughter. I wanted to provide her with
everything I did not have growing up.

My prayers through those tears were the only things that
saved me, and gave me the strength to handle everything thrown
my way. I felt as though I had no choice but to be father and
mother to my daughter, even though I could honestly be only one
or the other. The child needs the male/female example in their
lives to show them the nurturing that only the opposite sex can
provide. For me, my daughter had my father, her uncles, and a
select few of my male friends in her life to provide her the
attention she needed from a male, and the visual of how a male
should treat a female. Granted… I am nowhere near a perfect

mother, but I did my best and that is all that we all can do for our children. If there are dysfunctional aspects in your family life, then it is up to you to break the cycle, and change the habits from negative to positive.

Dysfunction comes from generational issues that have been repeated over and over, and as you know, we only do what we were taught growing up. Until we have experienced life through someone else's eyes, one who is a positive role model in our lives, we can only do what we know. For instance, saying "I love you" can be hard for some, because they have never heard their parents say those words, or give them a hug to show how much they care. Many people also settle for poor jobs or impoverished living arrangements, instead of pursuing their dreams for bigger and brighter opportunities. Sometimes you, as the next generation, have to break the cycle. This may mean to strive for a better paying job, higher education (college) and/or travel abroad. Allow yourself to dream and set goals, and go after them, despite your upbringing.

We put an enormous amount of stress on ourselves, trying to give our kids what we did not have. It is a generational thing, and one that gets more difficult to accomplish with each generation, but perhaps that drives us more to make it happen. We have to be careful that what we want for our children is not something too difficult for them to live up to. I am a firm believer in pushing my daughter to her greatest ability. Our kids are born with a blank slate, and can be anything that they may desire. It is up to us to give them every opportunity to learn about other cultures, languages, foods, and beliefs, so they develop into well-rounded adults. We get so busy with our daily lives that we forget that our children need to learn as much about being diverse as possible. Our past and present generations have had to deal with many struggles in relation to segregation, immigration, education shortfalls, declining communities, and economic struggles, to a point where they are not able to see the abundant opportunities available to them. Or they are unable to accept that they are worthy of such opportunities. So take time to open your eyes, mind, and hearts to see the possibilities that are out there for your children. If you struggle with certain subjects of your child's schoolwork, then find a tutor for that subject. Show your child that even though you may not know the answers, you keep looking for the answers and seek outside help to find them. Our children need to know that although we know a lot from our experiences in the world, we do not know it all. And researching the vast wealth of information that is found on the worldwide web, in our libraries, and in the people around us, is okay to do. And this should not be seen as a sign of weakness, but as a sign of strength.

Teen Years

Teen Years

Many people become single parents following situations that occur in high school, as teenagers may experience sex for the first time. In addition, they find themselves dealing with peer pressure and their own hormonal increases, juggling feelings of confusion, excitement, and fear of the unknown. The teen years are typically when the relationship between you and your teenager is tested. As our teens try to maneuver the process of transitioning from a child to a young adult, they are suddenly faced with feelings with which they are unfamiliar. This is the time many teens become rebellious, and push every button you have within you, and I do mean EVERY button. But this is also the time when they need their parents the most, as well as other supportive people in their lives. Always keep an honest, open door policy, which means you do not close the door when they tell you something that you do not want to hear. Opening and closing that door will make your teen clam up, and eventually refuse to tell you anything at all. Refusing to communicate can lead the teen into serious trouble, as they tend to seek out their peers for advice, who are also learning. This usually leads to bad advice and bad decisions. All I can say is that the high school years deserve more attention from parents, as well as teachers and the community. As single parents, we try to be there for our kids in all aspects of their lives, but we are only one person, and there will be times when we cannot be there. Those are the times when we are most vulnerable, and in danger of allowing our own guilt to attack us and drag us down the road of depression, all because we are trying to be everything to everybody. It's okay to admit we can't do it all. If our kids want to be involved in extracurricular activities, we should support them, but working a full-time job may require you to adjust your schedule so that you can be there for your kids. If not, make sure to have friends and family members who can be there until you can get a schedule change, or even a new job. For teens, knowing and seeing that their parents support what they are interested in is important! As a parent we have to remember that our teens are still learning who they are, even though they are more self-sufficient now. We may tend to rely on them more to assist around the house, or run errands once they have their driver's license. But they also need to experience being a teenager, instead of growing up too fast to fill in as your assistant or right-hand person. This is the time to rely upon your support system and family to assist you, so you can support your teen.

There's a fine line that you have to draw between being both your teen's friend and his or her parent. There are advantages and disadvantages to both, and this topic has spurred numerous discussions over the years. In my opinion, there is no right or wrong answer. Each child is different and one style of parenting does not work for everyone. We have to learn to adapt to the child to determine which direction is best for our personal

situation. Most importantly, we have to listen to our teens!
They are experiencing things in their generation that we did not
have to deal with, and it is harder to remain focused and not be
persuaded by their peers. Our teens need us more than ever to
understand them and what they are going through.

Bullying has been taken to a whole new level and many
teens choose to commit suicide to get out of the situation. As
their parents, we cannot tell our teens to just "grow up and deal
with it" or tell them "it is not that bad so get up and go to
school." Other teens are going on a killing rampage to get
revenge for bullying or rejection from their peers; and they have
even gone after their own parents and teachers. We must take
time out of our busy lives to listen to them, and give them our
undivided attention to make sure we understand what they are
telling us. How we handle our teens now will influence how
they will be as adults in the future.

Young Adult Years

Young Adult Years

By their young adult years, we hope our sons and daughters have retained everything that we have taught them, and actually use it. We want them to get an education and a good job to achieve their goals. Living in the real world, after high school has ended, is extremely difficult and is hard to teach to our young adults. They have to experience it and learn from their own mistakes. Now this is the most difficult part for single parents. How do you let go of your son or daughter after years of taking care of them and keeping them out of trouble? I have a very close relationship with my daughter and I wanted her to have an opportunity to achieve what I did not get to do. I wanted her to get her education early and learn to live on her own, so she would know that she could do it without having to rely upon a male companion.

Although she is getting her education early, she has experienced some real life ups and downs. It took a while for me to step back and let her fall without stepping in to pick up the pieces and fix things. I will not say that it was easy, because it certainly was not! I felt helpless watching her make decisions that I knew would not be good for her in the long run. I had to let go and let God take control, and prayed that she would fall back on everything that I taught her and make the right decisions. Our young adults are just like us when we were their age. They are curious and eager to figure out who they are and where they fit in. Each one wants to hurry up and move out of your home to be out in the world, so they do not have to answer to your rules anymore.

As I have said before, I would have stayed home a little longer, because the road of life is hard! Sometimes I wish I could go back to my parents' home, when there were no bills to pay and no real responsibilities with which I had to deal. We do not want our sons and daughters to make the same mistakes that we did because that was a hard road to travel, but some of them will go down that road in order to understand what they do not want out of life. Growing up is a journey. We all continue to make mistakes, but just as we learn from these mistakes, we should remember our young adults must do the same.

Everything goes back to making sure we, as the parent, actually take the time to listen to our children. I know how busy life can be, and we think we are listening to what they have to say when we are sort of listening and 'multi-tasking.' Actively listening to our young adults is a skill that I believe we all need to improve upon. If you only half-listen to them, then you may miss a crucial opportunity to help them through a sticky situation, and they may be hesitant to communicate with you in the future.

Married and Single

Parenting

Married and Single Parenting

The married and single parenting situation is a popular topic as well. Many women (and some men too) are married, but feel like they are single parents because their spouses are working overtime to provide for the family or traveling for business. They say when their spouse is home, they have to constantly ask for help around the house, taking out the trash, helping with the kids, and assisting with dinner. They feel as though they take care of everything, and no one appreciates them. They describe life as a never ending race to clean the house, wash clothes, work hard, get schoolwork done, baths done, food on the table, lunches made, kids to sporting events, church, yard work, and the list goes on. I have talked with several of my girlfriends who are experiencing this, and are frustrated at times when things become overwhelming. The frustration comes from doing everything that a single parent has to do, while knowing there is another adult in the household that should be helping out. My friends describe it as feeling like there's another kid to take care of, instead of a partner, when it comes to raising kids and taking care of everyday chores and business. Each person that I have spoken to has wanted the same thing: a marriage that is 50/50. If we look back on how we were raised, as little girls we were conditioned to be the nurturing ones. As women, we take care of the people we love. During the dating process, we seek the man's attention and love, so we do our best to be supportive and show them we care by cooking, giving advice, and being there to listen and encourage them. Little boys are raised to be strong, provide and protect the people they love. As men, they want to show the woman they are interested in that they can provide for them, so they work hard to get that good job, awesome car, nice clothes and extra money to take her out for a night on the town. They want to be there to fix whatever she needs and protect her from any harm.

Now in marriage, women expect the relationship to automatically shift from her doing everything to him taking on some of the responsibility. Many of my friends say they have voiced their frustrations to their spouses by saying, "this marriage is 50/50 and I need you to do your part!" But in order to have the relationship that you want in your marriage, you have to start the communication process early on, while you are dating. Both of you need to discuss what you expect in the relationship, and determine if you are on the same page as far as where you see your future going. All my friends who are happily married say that although they are happy, marriage is hard work, and takes a lot of communication. This does not mean talking at one another, but to each other, and actively listening to what they have to say. And that's advice all single people should adhere to, especially when dating.

Socializing and Sex

Socializing and Sex

If you are single, then you already know that trying to have a social life and raise kids is very challenging. The dating scene is difficult to manage without kids being involved. But with kids, we now have to think about if this person is good with kids, or making sure this person does not have violent tendencies. You do not want to introduce an abuser into your child's life. In the early years of my daughter's life, I felt uneasy dating, because I knew my daughter was not old enough to talk and tell me if something or someone harmed her. The possible guilt that I would feel if something happened to her would be unbearable. That little girl was my heart and I was very protective of her. Dating requires patience and careful decision-making in relation to whom we want to introduce to our kids. While dating, I chose not to bring any men around my daughter, simply because I was not sure if the relationship with the guy was serious enough to bring her into the picture. Plus, I knew that kids often attach themselves to anyone who shows them attention and kindness, especially if they feel this person can possibly be a dad or mom in their lives. If that happens and the relationship does not work out, how do you tell the child that this person will not be coming around anymore, and convince them it was not their fault. We walk a very fine line when it comes to trying to find a mate. I am no expert on this topic, nor do I claim

to be. I have come across men and women who are eagerly
seeking someone to help with the overwhelming load of raising
kids. We mistake our feelings toward a person who is saying
and doing the right things for love, but dismiss all the signs that
tells us the person is definitely not the right one, all because we
desperately want someone to carry the load even for a little
while. Do not make the critical error of allowing the person to
totally take over, or you may lose yourself in the situation. It is
easy to get lost in the emotions, as well as the temptation of
potential extra income and assistance with the bills or chores
around the house. You know what I mean... we become giddy,
and just the touch of the person sends us into la-la-land.   Those
feelings have a way of controlling us, but we have to remember
to stay in control of them. I have gotten so caught up in my
emotions that I placed everything on the back burner for a man,
including myself. I wanted to be held, taken care of, and feel
loved so badly that I put my education and my dreams aside to
experience it. Being in a relationship for the wrong reasons is an
opportunity to lose yourself in the moment. And though it takes
your mind off all the struggles at the time, it can cause more
problems than it's worth. Our kids depend on us, and we need to
make sure that we do not forget that when we are "so in love"
with the new person in our lives.

Another controversial issue is how much you involve the
right person in your life in the disciplining of your children. I
know from experience that as soon as the guy raised his voice at

my daughter, I went totally into protective mode and shut him down REAL quickly. As you can imagine, I gave him a piece of my mind, and when he told me, "you are being too soft with her," I totally lost it on him. Mommy mode kicked in and I told him to leave. We talked the next day after we both calmed down, but I realized that it would be difficult to have another person disciplining my daughter who was not family.

Each relationship is unique, and you have to decide for yourself if the person that you are introducing to your children is trustworthy enough to take on a disciplinary role in their lives. Something else to keep in mind when dating, is to truly get to know the person and determine if he or she really cares for children and would not do harm to them. By harm, I mean sexually, physically, and/or verbally abuse them. I wrestled with this while dating, because I knew that if any guy had harmed my daughter, there would be hell to pay! I do not like jail or prisons, but I would risk it to protect my daughter. I am sure you can relate to how I feel about guarding my most precious person in my life.

I am speaking from a single mother's view, but I know single fathers struggle with the same dating issues as well. You want to provide and protect your kids, as well as give them a mother figure in their lives. Yet, if the woman harmed your child in any way, you would also risk going to jail to protect them.

Another important topic is sex. It's a part of human nature, and a beautiful way to express your attraction toward another person. Many times sex is mistaken as love. For some who are starving for love, the act of sexual intercourse is taken as a form of "he loves me" instead of what it truly is… sex. As a single parent, you have to be cognizant of the difference between love and sex at all times. If not, you can find yourself in abusive situations that are difficult to escape. Those relationships are not healthy for you, and definitely not appropriate for your child. So take a moment to make sure you're seeing the relationship for what it is before you involve your children in something that can be emotionally detrimental to them. If you need to, seek professional counseling or other professional assistance to help you get back on track to parenting in a healthy way.

To manage your way through parenthood, you will need help from several areas of your life.

You need to seek assistance from family, friends and other single parents in your community. Keep an open mind to alternative ways to teach your children, and learn how to explain things to them. You will be surprised at what questions your kids will ask, and at what moment they will ask you. You know the saying, "kids say the darndest thing?" Well it's true in more ways than one. So take advantage of your support groups to learn different parenting survival tips from each other.

Tips for Survival

Tips for Survival

Seek out those who are one or two levels higher than you and ask for advice or mentoring. You cannot learn from someone who has not been where you are or doesn't know what you have been through. You need to learn from people who are where you want to be, and find out how they reached their goals, which will force you to look at your life and make necessary changes. I remember having to step back and look at the people who surrounded me in my life. I had to weed through the negative minded people, those who voiced I could not achieve anything more than being a mom and providing for my daughter. They could not get past the struggles in life to see the benefits.

All of this negativity in my life brought negative thoughts into my mind and how I saw my future. I began to believe that I was not going to make much of myself as well. After reading "In the Meantime" by Iyanla Vanzant, I did the personal work of weeding through my life and cleaning out my closet, and came to see that I was and am worth it, and I will be successful at whatever I put my mind to. So I say to you... know that you can achieve your goals as long as you believe in yourself. Remove the negative people and conversations from your life, and watch the doors open for you.

Having positive role models in your life gives you an additional boost to continue through your personal struggles, because you have a person who can keep you on a positive track.

Single parenting requires a strong, inner motivation to keep pushing forward, and that is why you have to find ways to inspire yourself. I would read books or listen to church sermons to help me to understand the feelings I was experiencing, and work through them until I could see the light at the end of the tunnel. Also, make sure you keep yourself at the top of the "to do" list. Start with something small, like taking a quiet, hot bath, if only for fifteen to twenty minutes. In our busy and hectic lives, those few minutes mean everything. It might seem selfish, but taking a personal day from work just to concentrate on yourself is a great idea. Take advantage of the time your child is cared for in daycare! If you are sleep deprived, then having a day to yourself to catch up on rest and chores is wonderful. I have done this numerous times and it has been a blessing for me and my sanity. Let's face it… sanity is the one thing that we have to hold on to while raising our kids!

Raising kids solo means a lot of emotional rollercoaster moments. Do not hold your emotions in, because this will only add to your building tension, and it will eventually backfire on you. Take time to release your emotions by crying, exercising, and anything that will not land you in trouble with the law. I had to learn to forgive myself as well, and I suggest that you do the same. I had to look back on my life and forgive myself for all the moments I doubted myself. The times when I felt ashamed and sorry for myself, or for the bad decisions I made, and the guilt I felt when I couldn't afford things for my daughter. I also envied those who had what I so desperately wanted. I am not a perfect person or parent, and I, too, made mistakes while raising my daughter the best way I knew possible. I cannot turn back the hands of time, but I can learn from my faults and help my daughter avoid the same.

My final tip is to love yourself, because if you cannot do that, it will be difficult to love someone else. How can you show love if you do not love all aspects of you? When your first child is born, you start to truly understand what unconditional love is, and how to give love unconditionally. Seeing my daughter for the first time in the hospital brought out a deep feeling of love that I did not realize I could feel. You know that feeling that I am talking about, right? You have to raise your kids to the best of your ability, with the help and support of the people around you. Remember to continue to work on yourselves as you prepare your kids for their futures, for they will need you more than ever in this ever changing world. Keep the lines of communication open with them, and truly stop to listen to what they are telling you, instead of assuming that you already know.

Life is too short and precious, so make sure you enjoy all the great moments in your child's life, because they grow up fast. Many times it was the small things that touched my heart, such as having a hard day at work and arriving home to my daughter's outstretched arms, waiting to give me a huge hug and just wanting to be held by mom. This melted my heart and made the stress of the day slowly disappear.

Encouragement

Encouragement

You must be very proud of yourself for taking on the responsibility of raising your child on your own. Although there will be hard times when you feel you cannot go on, you must push forward and have confidence in yourself that you are strong enough to do it. Fall back onto your faith, and believe with all of your heart and soul that God will always be there with you, and would not put more upon you than you can handle. I can't tell you how many times I've fallen to my knees and prayed for direction and strength to keep pushing forward.

Our children are worth every bit of the struggles and challenges that we have to face. Parenting is a privilege and we must not take it for granted. We have been given this opportunity to be a parent/ guardian to our precious little ones. So many single parents have raised their children before you, so remember you can do it, too. You need to stay positive and surround yourself with people who believe in you and what you can achieve. Don't be so proud that you miss out or turn down assistance from others. I was so blessed to have people in my life that I could reach out to and talk about my problems with, and receive excellent advice. That's not to say that I didn't get bad advice. But at least I was able to recognize most of it for what it was.

You are a strong person who can push through the tough times and reach your personal goals. Be a great role model for your child so they know how to be a good parent to their own kids one day. I went back to school to get my Bachelors and Master's degrees, while my daughter was in high school. We did our homework together, and she could see that if I could reach my goals, then she could too! Today, I'm so proud of my daughter, as she will be completing her Masters degree this year. She has big goals that she wants to achieve, and she has the motivation and drive to accomplish them all. So remember that your little ones are always watching what you do, and it's up to you to guide them to become great, responsible adults. You got this - so be the best parent that you can be! **Always remember to challenge, love, inspire, motivate and believe (C.L.I.M.B.) in yourself!**

Notes

Notes

www.ingramcontent.com/pod-product-compliance
Lightning Source LLC
Chambersburg PA
CBHW031522040426
42445CB00009B/348